Charles Tupper

Annual Statement Respecting the Canadian Pacific Railway

Charles Tupper

Annual Statement Respecting the Canadian Pacific Railway

ISBN/EAN: 9783337307899

Printed in Europe, USA, Canada, Australia, Japan

Cover: Foto ©ninafisch / pixelio.de

More available books at **www.hansebooks.com**

SPEECH

OF

SIR CHARLES TUPPER

ON THE

CANADIAN PACIFIC RAILWAY

RESOLUTIONS,

FEBRUARY 5TH, 1884.

Sir *Charles Tupper* moved, that The House do go into Committee of the Whole, on *Tuesday, next,* to take into consideration that portion of the Speech from the Throne at the opening of the present Session in which His Excellency informs us that His Government has thought it of the greatest importance for the settlement of the North-West and the development of our trade that the completion of the Canadian Pacific Railway from sea to sea should be hastened, and the Company enabled to open the line throughout by the spring of 1886 ; that with this view, and in order to aid the Company in procuring sufficient capital for the purpose by the disposal of its unsold shares, the Government agreed to receive a deposit of money and securities sufficient to pay a minimum three per cent. dividend for ten years on sixty-five millions of the stock, that arrangement being made in the belief that it would give steadiness and increased value to the shares on the market ; that a combination of unfavourable circumstances has prevented the fulfilment of these expectations, and the Company has not been able to obtain the required capital by a sale of its stock ; and that the best means of preventing any delay in the great object of the early completion of the railway demands our earnest consideration : And to consider the following Resolutions :—

1. *Resolved*, That the Government may return to the Company the securities now held under the third section of the Act 44 *Victoria*, Chapter 1, intituled, *An Act respecting the Canadian Pacific Railway*, and under the second section of the construction contract referred to in the said Act.

2. *Resolved*, That the money subsidy hereafter payable to the Company, may be paid as the work on either the Central or Eastern Section of the Railway proceeds, in the proportion which the value of the work done on such section, and for which payment is demanded, bears to the value of the whole work remaining to be done, under the contract, on such section.

3. *Resolved*, That the time for the payment by the Company of the sum of Two Millions Eight Hundred and Fifty three Thousand Nine Hundred and Twelve Dollars ($2,853,912) agreed by the said Company to be paid on or before the First day of February, One Thousand Eight Hundred and Eighty-four (1884) as part of the fund referred to in their agreement with the Government of the Seventh day of November last, shall be extended to the Seventh day of November, One Thousand Eight Hundred and Eighty-eight (1888), when the sum of Four Million Five Hundred and Twenty-seven Thousand Dollars ($4,527,000) being the last instalment of the said fund payable by the Company to the Government will fall due, the whole with interest payable half yearly at the rate of four per centum per annum as agreed upon at the time of the execution of the said agreement, and that the same shall then be paid to the Government, together with the said last mentioned amount; forming together the sum of Seven Million Three Hundred and Eighty Thousand Nine Hundred and Twelve Dollars ($7,380,912), bearing interest at the said last mentioned rate until paid.

4. *Resolved*, That the Government may, out of any unappropriated moneys forming part of the Consolidated Revenue Fund of Canada, make a loan to the said Company of an amount in money, not exceeding Twenty-two Million Five Hundred Thousand Dollars ($22,500,000) to be repaid to the Government on or before the first day of May, One Thousand Eight Hundred and Ninety-one- (1891), with interest at the rate of five per centum per annum, payable half yearly, until full payment of the principal; and that as part of the said loan the Government may pay to the Company forthwith, such amount not exceeding Seven Million Five Hundred Thousand Dollars, ($7,500,000) as shall be required by the Company to extinguish its present floating debt, the amount of such debt to be established to

the satisfaction of the Government: and that the remainder of the said loan shall be paid to the Company as the work of construction proceeds, in the same proportion as that which is hereby provided for the payment of the balance of the money subsidy.

5. *Resolved*, That as security for the repayment of the said loan, with interest as aforesaid, and as additional security for the payment of the said sum of Seven Million Three Hundred and Eighty Thousand Nine Hundred and Twelve Dollars ($7,380,912) and interest, falling due on the Seventh day of November, One Thousand Eight Hundred and Eighty-eight (1888), the Government shall have a first lien and charge upon the entire property of the Company real and personal, now owned or hereafter to be acquired or owned by them, including their main line of Railway, the extensions thereof, their branch lines of Railway, the whole of their equipment, rolling stock and plant, and including all steamers and vessels; and also upon the land grant of the Company, earned and to be hereafter earned ; saving always, however, the rights of the holders of the existing mortgages on the extensions of the line of the Railway from Callander to Brockville and Montreal, as security for the unpaid balances of the purchase money of the lines constituting the said extensions; and subject to the mortgage upon the land grant, executed by the Company to secure their issue of land grant bonds, That the Government shall continue to hold and retain the entire amount of land grant bonds now in its custody or possession, subject to redemption under the terms of the said land grant mortgage, and with all remedies as to interest, voting power and all other matters in respect thereof, which would be held or possessed, or could be exercised by any purchaser of the said bonds : That all moneys received by the Government from the Trustees of the Land Grant Bonds in redemption of such bonds shall be applied as follows, that is to say: All moneys so received in respect of ten million dollars of the said bonds shall be applied: *Firstly*, in extinction of the interest accrued and due upon the said loan, and upon the said sum of Seven Million Three Hundred and Eighty Thousand Nine Hundred and Twelve Dollars ($7,380,912). *Secondly*, on account of the capital of the said sum of Seven Million Three Hundred and Eighty Thousand Nine Hundred and Twelve Dollars ($7,380,912), and *Thirdly*, on account of the capital of the said loan :—And that the Government may make such arrangements as it shall deem expedient, for securing the payment to it, after the redemption of the land grant bonds, of the proceeds of all sales of lands granted or to be granted to the Company under the contract,

1½

to be applied to the purposes and in the order aforesaid. And that the remaining five million dollars of land grant bonds and money received from the said Trustees in redemption thereof, shall continue to be held on the conditions and for the purposes mentioned in the said contract.

6. *Resolved,* That the Government shall cause a deed of agreement to be executed by the Company, and on behalf of the Government, providing for such remedies, terms, and conditions for securing the application of the said loan to the purposes for which the same is hereby authorized, and the repayment of the said loan, and of the said sum of Seven Million Three Hundred and Eighty Thousand Nine Hundred and Twelve Dollars ($7,380,912) the whole with interest (including interest on any interest in default) ; for the release of the said lien and charge upon such repayment ; for continuing the sale and realization of the value of the said lands, after the redemption of the land grant bonds,—the payment to the Government of the proceeds of such sales, and the discharge of such lands from the said charge upon payment of the price of sale thereof; as the Government shall deem expedient, such price not to be less than one dollar and twenty-five cents per acre :—

Provided always that, among such remedies, terms and conditions, it shall be agreed and provided, that upon default for twelve months in the payment of any half yearly instalment of interest upon the said loan, or upon the said sum of Seven Million Three Hundred and Eighty Thousand Nine Hundred and Twelve Dollars, or either of them, or in the payment of the principal of either of the said sums,when the same shall become due, in accordance with the provisions hereof, the right of the Company under their contract hereinbefore mentioned, to demand or receive any further cash or land subsidy shall cease and determine, and the said Railway and extensions thereof, branches, equipment, rolling stock, plant, including steamers, and all lands and property of the Company and all land grant bonds then in the possession of the Government shall upon the occurrence and continuance for the said period of twelve months of such default, *ipso facto,* and without any notice or proceeding whatsoever, vest in Her Majesty, and shall forthwith, thereupon, be taken possession of by the Minister of Railways and Canals, on behalf of the Government of Canada, and each and every employee of the Company shall, from and after the expiry of the said period of twelve months, become and be the employee of the Government during pleasure, and shall hold and possess any matter or thing appertaining to the said Company then in his custody,

5

as and for the Government; and the rates of interest, and the terms of payment hereby fixed, shall not be disturbed or altered by the terms of such agreement.

7. *Resolved*, That the said Company be authorized to execute an agreement of the nature and purport hereinbefore provided for, and to charge its entire property and assets, in manner and form as hereinbefore described; and in such agreement to agree upon such further and other conditions as the Government may prescribe; provided that authority to accept the provisions of the Act to be passed in this behalf, and to the Board of Directors of the Company to execute an agreement containing the charges upon the said Railway and property and the other conditions required or authorized by such Act, shall be granted by the share-holders of the Company, either by a resolution passed at a special general meeting of such shareholders, called for the purpose, by a vote of at least two-thirds in value of such of the shareholders as shall be present or represented at such meeting, or by an instrument or instruments executed by at least two-thirds in value of the whole of the shareholders of the Company, in person or represented by their attorneys or proxies respectively duly authorized in that behalf.

8. *Resolved*, That until the payment in full of the indebted-ness of the Company to the Government with interest, all moneys earned and to be earned by the Company as postal subsidy and for transport service shall be retained by the Government and shall be applied on account of the interest to become due from time to time upon the loan hereby authorized, and then to the payment of the principal.

9. *Resolved*, That the stock of the Company, amounting to Thirty-five Million Dollars ($35,000,000), now in the hands of the Government, shall be held by the Minister of Finance, and may be sold by the Company, with the consent of the Government, on condition that the proceeds of such sale, less the amount required to be paid to the Government to secure a half-yearly dividend thereon, at the rate of three per centum per annum, up to the Seventeenth (17th) day of August, One Thousand Eight Hundred and Ninety-three (1893) inclusive, shall be applied, under the direction of the Government, either to the improvement or extension of the Railway, or its equipment, or to the repayment of the indebtedness of the Company to the Government; and that if at any time the stock of the Company should reach a price which, in the opinion of the Government, would render it expedient to sell the said stock, or any part thereof, then and thereupon, on notice being given to the Company by the Government, requiring that the said stock, or any part

thereof, be sold, and specifying the minimum price at which the same shall be so sold, the Company shall cause the same to be offered for sale, and sold in conformity with such notice ; and in default of their doing so, within a reasonable delay (which delay shall be in the discretion of the Government) the Government shall have the right to sell the same or any part thereof at or above such minimum price, and shall apply the proceeds thereof as it is herein provided such proceeds shall be applied in the event of the sale of such stock by the Company.

10. *Resolved*, That so long as the said several sums of money loaned as aforesaid or any part thereof, or the interest thereon remain unpaid, no mortgage, lien or charge of any description shall be created upon the Railway, property or assets of the Company, or any part thereof; nor shall any stock be issued by the Company, pending such repayment, above or beyond the amount of One Hundred Million Dollars ($100,000,000) to which the same is now limited.

11. *Resolved*, That legislative provision be made for giving effect to the said Resolutions, and that the mover thereof have leave to bring in a Bill for that purpose.

CANADIAN PACIFIC RAILWAY.

Sir CHARLES TUPPER. Mr. Speaker, in moving that the House resolve itself into Committee of the Whole on the proposed Resolutions respecting the Canadian Pacific Railway, I desire to make a general statement as to the position of that great work. I am deeply impressed with the importance of the decision at which the House may arrive in regard to the Resolutions that I now have the honour to propose. A year ago, when discharging a somewhat similar duty, making a statement to the House in regard to the position that the Canadian Pacific Railway then occupied, I ventured to say that the most sanguine expectations of the promoters of that great enterprise in Parliament had been more than realized; that the work performed by the Canadian Pacific Railway Company had been unprecedented in regard to the vigour with which it had been prosecuted, and the success that had attended their efforts. I am glad, Sir, to be able on the present occasion to reiterate that statement, and to say that the position occupied in respect to the progress of that great work is still stronger, still greater, to-day, than it was when I made that statement a year ago. At that time I ventured to affirm that if the Canadian Pacific Railway Company made the same progress in the future that they had made in the past, we had

every reason to believe that the line would be open from
ocean to ocean by the end of 1886. In consequence
the unabated vigour and the increased energy with which
that work has been pushed, I am glad to say that if
in the future the same progress is made as in the
past, we shall be able to shorten the period for its
completion by something like a year; that it is now
believed to be quite practicable to complete the whole
of that great enterprise by the end of the year
1885, and open the line for travel and traffic in
the spring of 1886. I need not say, Sir, to the House
that those who have watched the progress of that work,
as I am sure every hon. member of this House has
done, will feel the immense importance to this country of
that which is practicable being realized at the earliest possible day. The contract entered into less than three years
ago—because it is not quite three years since Parliament ratified the contract made with the Canadian Pacific
Railway Company—provided that the Government should
complete 428 miles of road from Port Arthur to Red
River, and 213 miles from Port Moody to Kamloops, a
total of 641 miles, by the time stated in the contracts for
their completion, which was July, 1885. I am glad to be
able to say that that which the Government undertook to
do in relation to the portions of the work that still remained
under construction by the Government will be fully realized.
As I stated to the House when last addressing it upon this
subject, in order to open the line for traffic in the spring
of last year, it became necessary to transfer to the Canadian
Pacific Railway Company a portion of the work which
remained to be done on contracts 41 and 42, and work which
required to be performed on contracts 13 and 25, being the
first section from Port Arthur, in consequence of the long
period that had elapsed after the road was completed, the
work required to be executed in order to place it in the
condition in which the Government agreed to hand it over
to the Canadian Pacific Railway Company. I stated to the
House that it was intended to transfer those works to the
Canadian Pacific Railway Company in order that the road
might be operated at the same time that the works
of completion were in progress, and as the only practical
means by which that important result could be attained. Those arrangements, as you, Sir, are aware from
the contract which I have laid on the Table, were carried
out. The Canadian Pacific Railway Company took over
all the works requiring to be done by the contractors of
section 42 at the prices contained in their contract, less 15
per centum on the train work that the former contractors had

undertaken and proposed to do, and to which, as it lessened the cost of the work which was to be done, the Government and the Company both agreed the contractors were entitled as a matter of justice. That work has consequently been completed, or is being completed by the Canadian Pacific Railway Company upon the same terms as it would have been completed, and at the same cost to the country, under the contract that had been made with the contractors for section 42. The portion of the work that remained to be executed on sections 13, 25 and 41 was also agreed to be done by that Company upon the lowest terms, and at prices which similar work had cost in connection with those contracts. The sum of $286,000 has been paid in relation to that work performed by the Canadian Pacific Railway Company entirely outside of their contract for the whole line. I may mention here that I do not take that question into consideration at all, because that contract with the Company is precisely in the same position as contracts with any other private individuals or contractors, and has no relation to the question we are now about to discuss. I may say in reference to the works upon the 213 miles from Port Moody to Kamloops, that the progress has been of the most satisfactory character. As the House is well aware, the contractors for those 213 miles were Mr. Mills and Mr. Onderdonk, the latter being engaged in both. On something over $9,000,000 of an estimate for the work on that section over $7,000,000 have already been executed, and with the force at their command and the progress they are making, we have every assurance that the work will be completed within the time stated in the contract; in fact the track will be laid from Port Moody to Kamloops, through the whole distance in September next; and within the time—and I think I might say considerably before the time—named in the contract the entire works will be completed. I am glad, Sir, to be able to say that the further information which we have acquired, down to the present time, when, as I have already stated, over $7,000,000 of the $9,000,000 proposed expenditure has been completed, shows that the cost of that work will not exceed the estimate which I have already given to the House. Then, Sir, the Company were bound under the terms of the contract to construct 650 miles from Callander to Port Arthur, and also to construct a line from Red River to Kamloops, a distance which by the present line is ascertained to be about 1,250 miles, making 1,900 miles in all, as nearly as possible. Trains are now running on 1,131 miles, although it is not yet three years since Parliament ratified the contract under which they are working. These facts have reference to the main line;

but the Company have also constructed 239 miles of branches on which trains are running, making now in operation of main line and branches no less than 1,370 miles. A large amount of work has also been executed upon 160 miles of the line (in addition to the 1,131 miles) of the very heavy works north of Lake Superior. The Company have at this moment over 9,000 men employed in the construction of the portion of the line that remains to be completed in that region ; and, as I have already stated, with the force at their command, and the appliances with which they are prepared to execute the work, we have every reason to believe that it is entirely practicable to complete the Canadian Pacific Railway from end to end by the close of the year 1885. Now, Sir, I may say with reference to the character of the work, that when the contract was entered into with the Canadian Pacific Railway Company, it was feared by some gentlemen in this House that a sufficiently high standard was not created whereby the Government would secure the construction of that work in as perfect and thorough a manner as it was desirable it should be constructed. My answer to those criticisms was that as they were constructing it for themselves, and as the cost of operating the line for all time to come would depend on the mode in which the work was performed, we had in these facts a better guarantee than any possible standard of construction, that the work would be well executed. I think, Sir, it is not necessary for me to say to this House that the manner in which the Canadian Pacific Railway Company have executed the work which they have performed is so satisfactory as to command, as it has commanded, the unqualified approval and admiration of every person who has visited and inspected this road and who knows anything of railway construction either in the adjoining States or in Canada. A great number of gentlemen, thoroughly qualified to judge of the quality of railway works, have gone over the line, and from them there has been but one opinion, and that opinion is that not only has the contract been fully and faithfully carried out but that it has been exceeded in every particular, and that on any part of this continent there is not to be found a better road running through a similar country. The Chief Engineer of the Canadian Pacific Railway has visited the works from time to time, and he affirms, in the fullest possible manner, as also does Mr. Sandford Fleming, formerly Chief Engineer of the Canadian Pacific Railway, that it would be impossible to find a work executed in a more satisfactory manner than this work has been by the Canadian Pacific Railway Company. It might, perhaps, be desirable for me to give a slight glance at the character of the work which remains to be done. From Sudbury Junction to Michipicoton the work is said to be light, the grading for the greater part is of a sandy nature ; this distance is 210 miles. On the 140 miles from Michipicoton to Pic, the work is said to be moderately light, the cuttings generally of clay or sand with some rock. From Pic to within 35 miles of Nepigon, the work is excessively heavy, the grading being composed chiefly of hard rock ; distance 95 miles. It is upon this heavy work, to a very large extent, that the strong force which I mentioned are now concentrating their efforts. The work for the remaining 35 miles to Nepigon is moderately light ; the grading is about completed. Then, as regards the work in the Rocky Mountains, from the summit of the Rocky Mountains to the foot of the Mountains, the work may be classed as generally heavy, with some short distances very heavy ; distance, 45 miles. From the foot of the Rocky Mountains to the foot of Seikirk Mountain the work is described as being light, the country being flat ; distance, 30 miles. From the eastern foot of the Selkirk Mountain to the mouth of Eagle Pass, the work may be considered moderate for mountain work, the grading being largely through gravel ; distance, 64 miles. The remaining distance from the mouth of Eagle Pass to Kamloops, 161 miles, is described as medium, the cuttings being rock, clay and gravel. This makes in all 780 miles remaining to be constructed north of Lake Superior and the part to connect the end of the track at the summit of the Rocky Mountains with the works which are in progress by the Government at Kamloops. The summit of the Rocky Mountains is 5,300 feet, and of the Selkirk Mountain, 4,316 feet. I may say, Sir, that down to the present hour the Canadian Pacific Railway Company have prosecuted their work with unabated vigour, and have, so far as carrying out the contract into which they entered with the Government is concerned, left no ground of complaint as to the mode in which they have proceeded. It is well known, Sir, to the House that in October last the Company applied to the Government for the purpose of obtaining their support to guarantee the interest on the outstanding stock of the Company— some $65,000,000. The first proposal, as the House is aware, was to obtain a guarantee on the whole $100,000,000 of stock issued, and it was supposed by the Company at that time—in fact, I believe they had reason to suppose—that no difficulty would be experienced in obtaining the amount of money necessary to guarantee the payment of a $

per cent. dividend on the whole of their stock, the entire \$100,000,000. That was subsequently found to be impracticable, and an amended proposition was submitted to limit the guarantee to all the outstanding stock, the \$65,000,000, and to provide that the remaining \$35,000,000 should be deposited with the Government, and no more stock issued except as the Company deposited the money necessary to furnish the guarantee of 3 per cent. It will not be necessary for me to discuss at any length the reasons which obliged the Company to adopt the course they did. It is perfectly familiar to the House that a demoralization in railway stocks occurred in New York in regard to all the trans-continental lines of railway, and everything connected with them, which rendered it impossible for the Company to sell the remaining stock—upon which they depended to obtain the money to complete the Canadian Pacific Railway with the promptness and vigour with which they were performing that work—except at a ruinous sacrifice. I do not intend, Sir, on the present occasion, to go at length into the causes that especially affected the Canadian Pacific Railway. I want, in making a calm, dispassionate, business statement of the position of that great work, and of the question as it now stands before this House—I want to avoid, as far as possible, raising any matter of a controversial character. But, Sir, I may say to the House, what is very well known, that in the United States, parties connected with the Northern Pacific Railway, the Central Pacific Railway, and the Union Pacific Railway—in fact, all the trans-continental lines of railway—parties, who a few years ago regarded the proposal to construct a Canadian Pacific Railway by the people of the Dominion as entirely illusory, and as a matter that need give them little concern—have gradually, but latterly very rapidly, been changing their opinions with regard to that great work. They have found that the vigour with which the work has been prosecuted has rendered the early completion of the Canadian Pacific Railway a question far removed from the region of the merely theoretical; and, Sir, they have learned, upon enquiry and examination, when their attention was drawn to the subject, that Canada possesses advantages with respect to a trans-continental railway that would render it a formidable rival, either of the Northern Pacific, or the Union Pacific and Central Pacific Railway. And the result of the discovery of the greater advantages which a Canadian Pacific line of railway would possess, has been a great increase in the active hostility of all the trans-continental lines of railway— and, I may say, of all the lines in the United States con.

nected with those trans-continental lines—towards the Canadian project. And, Sir, I wish I was able to say that the hostility to this great national work—for national work it is—was confined to those lines of railway that might be considered rival lines in a foreign country. I say, I wish I was able to say that the Canadian Pacific Railway Company and this great national enterprise had not suffered from any hostility within, as well as without, our borders. But, Sir, it is well known that attempts to decry this great work, attempts to break down this great enterprise—aye, Sir, even if it involved breaking Canada down, as far as possible, along with it—have been entered upon, not only in the New York, but in the London markets, with very determined vigour; but, as I said before—and I do not intend to detain the House longer on that subject—the result is well known —the value of the Canadian Pacific Railway stock became so impaired and weakened as to render it impossible for the Company to obtain money from that source sufficient to enable them to prosecute to rapid completion their great enterprise. Now, Sir, the House will remember that when Parliament was providing for the means of constructing this great work, the Government who submitted the proposition to the House were told that we were granting an unduly large subsidy for its accomplishment. We were told that, in addition to the work we were performing to cost $28,000,000, we were giving $25,000,000 in money, and an inordinate quantity of land, when we added a grant of 25,000,000 acres, as so great a subvention was not necessary in order to provide fully for the completion of the work. Well, Sir, that land was estimated—I think I may say without much controversy—as worth about $2 an acre. Assuming, therefore, that that was all true, it would involve to the people of Canada, for the construction of the Canadian Pacific Railway, a cost of $103,000,000. But our answer was this—and it has been thoroughly established by subsequent experience—that great as was the quantity, valuable as was the character of those lands, valuable as they would be rendered by the construction of this great line of railway and the branches which the Company proposed to construct in connection with it, it would not be possible for them to realize from those lands the money that would be required to carry on the work. That, Sir, has been abundantly borne out by the facts. With every effort that was possible being made to realize on the lands, the time came when it was apparent that, great as was the value of the property of the Company, it would be impossible alone by issuing the stock of the Company, to obtain the means to carry on the work. As I

13

stated before, the resources of the Company became impaired, and if they threw the additional $35,000,000 of their stock on the market, it would be sacrificed without their obtaining the means expected. Now, Sir, it will not be neces. sary, with the papers before you, for me to refer to the mode in which the dividends guaranteed on the stock were provided. You are aware that the Company provided $8,710,240 in cash, and you are aware that they provided for the payment of all the remaining money required to warrant the Government in giving the guarantee, by securities of the most ample description. I do not think there is any person in this House or out of it, who will be disposed to question the desirability, on the part of the Government, of securing the prompt completion of this great work, by giving their assistance in the form that was proposed. The Government has scarcely transcended the usual borrowing powers of a Government. So far as the $8,710,240 providing a guarantee for five years was concerned, of course no question can arise. That was entirely within the borrowing powers of the Government,—although requiring the approval of this House, and one which the Government felt every confidence in asking this House to approve — to accept undoubted securities for the payment of a portion of that money at a deferred period; thus enabling; as was to be desired, this work to be prosecuted with the same vigour as that which had hitherto characterized its construction. There is another point to which I might be expected to draw the attention of the House for a few moments in connection with the guarantee, and that is that in addition to the land grant bonds that were deposited to secure payment of the entire amount required to provide the guarantee for the whole ten years for which the Government became responsible, a postal subsidy estimated at $3,000,000 was taken as a part security. I am quite certain those who will take the trouble to look into that question will find that the Government were amply warranted in doing this—that in fact it was no novelty to use a postal subsidy in that way. It was known that we were paying at the same rate to the Canadian Pacific Railway, as to other railways, a large postal subsidy; and that in a very short time, assuming the work to be completed, and even in the absence of the completion of the work, we should be paying over $120,000 a year for postal subsidy, which would represent the $3,000,000 that were taken as a security, without regard to the transport service they would perform for the Department of the Interior in connection with the management of Indian Affairs and the Mounted

Police. But, I say, altogether apart from that, it is known
that, at the same rate paid to other railways, they will
become entitled to a subsidy of no less than $204,000 a year
for the transmission of mails on the completion of the road,
representing at an early day a much greater amount than
the $3,000,000 that was estimated to be covered. Taking the
second lien upon the $5,000,000 of bonds deposited with the
Government to secure the operation of the line for ten years—
and as I shall show by-and-bye a security that certainly we now
know never will be required to be called into operation, and a
first lien upon a further sum of $3,250,000 in bonds—abundant
security was taken, independently of the postal subsidy, for
the entire amount that the Government were required to
guarantee. It thus became a question with the Government
whether this guarantee should be given for the purpose, not
of enabling the Canadian Pacific Railway to complete their
contract—I wish the House to understand at the very outset
that no change is proposed by the Canadian Pacific Railway
Company in regard to their contract—that the Canadian
Pacific Railway Company, taking into account the property
they own, the lands that they possess—putting a more moderate estimate of value upon them than that of hon. gentlemen
opposite, and one in which I think the House will be prepared to concur—putting the most moderate estimate on
the value of their lands, the Canadian Pacific Railway Company feel that they are able to carry their contract to completion without the alteration of a letter. There is no proposal now submitted to the House to change a single line of
the contract with the Canadian Pacific Railway. It is to
stand now as it stood on the first day when we laid it on
the Table of the House. Instead of its value having
decreased, every one knows that with every suc-
ceeding year the Canadian Pacific Railway has
established itself in a stronger and stronger position.
Every one knows that the experience in the sale of a portion of their lands—between three and four millions of
acres already sold by the Company—leaves no room to
doubt that in that subvention they have ample means for
the completion of the work, with the additional means
which they themselves have already provided in connection
with its progress and construction, but the question that
is submitted for the consideration of the House, and that
was submitted for the consideration of the Government
when the Company asked for this guarantee by the Government, upon depositing money and securities to represent
every dollar of it, was whether that step should be taken,
not to enable the Canadian Pacific Railway to fulfil their
obligations and to carry out the contract they had

made with the Government, but for the purpose of anticipating the time provided in that contract by over five years. The Government believed they were consulting the best interests of Canada in adopting measures which, without cost and risk to the country, would accomplish so great and desirable an object as that of opening to the people of this country all that trans-continental line of communication from end to end in that brief period. It is well known that the Northern Pacific Railway Company, by making a great effort, have completed their line running from Lake Superior to the Pacific Ocean. It is well known that traffic once established in a groove is very difficult to be drawn from it and placed upon another line: and we regarded it,therefore, as the first consideration in the interests of the country—looking at this as a great trans-continental line of railway—that at the earliest possible moment there should be a line of communication for travel and traffic extending across this Continent on Canadian territory, and enabled to draw to its support all that travel and all that traffic which could possibly be drawn to it from our own country and the country which lies to the south of us. Under these circumstances, the Government adopted, with some modifications, the proposals made by the Company and provided for the guarantee. I need not tell the House that it resulted in failure—that all the expectations that the Company had formed, and that the Government had formed—and I am able to say capitalists without exception in Canada, in the United States and in England,had formed—to the effect that the result of that guarantee would be to give all the means required by the Company to enable them to carry on their work with such vigour and promptness as would secure its completion by the end of 1885, signally failed. They were found to be erroneous. But if the Company were wrong, if the Government were wrong, the error was one in which financial men and capitalists without exception on both sides of the Atlantic shared, because no doubt was entertained as to what the result would be. The war, however, against transcontinental railway stock was intensified, the efforts to bear the stock of the Canadian Pacific Railway were intensified, and then the result was that the project ended in signal failure—not only in failure but in disaster. Because, as it will be readily seen, the Company found themselves in this position: that having failed to obtain such increased value for their stock, as every person supposed they would obtain, they were left without the $8,710,240 of their cash deposited with the Government, an amount locked up which otherwise they would have had at their command for the purpose of going on with the construction of the line. So that instead of obtaining the object expected, the very contrary occurred, and the embarrassment and difficulty that had before been experienced by them in providing for a rapid and vigourous completion of the line was intensified. Under these circumstances, the Government submit the Resolutions that are now on the Table for the consideration of this House. And I think, after I have had an opportunity of placing in the most frank and open manner before the House all the questions connected with this Company, every transaction so far as I am able to judge that is interesting to this House in regard to their position, that the House will come to the conclusion that the Government are not only warranted in submitting, but that they would fail in their duty to the House and to the country if they did not submit the propositions that are now placed before you, not with a view to enable the Canadian Pacific Railway Company to derive advantage, or to realize larger returns for the property that they possess, but for the purpose of enabling the people of Canada to have finished within two years this great trans-continental line of railway, and to derive all the advantages that are calculated to flow from the prompt and vigorous completion of this work. Now, Sir, the Company ask that we should postpone, or rather I should say that the Resolutions before you ask that the Company may postpone, the payment of $7,380,912 for the guarantee for five years. But they leave with the Government ample security, as provided for under the original arrangement, for that postponement. Practically the proposal before the House is only a change of the payment of the $2,853,912 that was to be paid on the first day of this month. That is the change from the arrangement already made in relation to the guarantee. It is proposed to postpone the payment of that guarantee for five years, and to loan the Company $22,500,000, to be repaid on the first day of May, 1891. The conditions of that advance may briefly be stated as follows: In the first place, it is proposed that in future the payment for work done shall be placed upon a different basis from that which was contained in the contract. That is not a real but simply a nominal change in the terms of the contract. When the contract was made, it was provided that, upon the completion of every 20 miles, the Company should receive payment, according to the terms of the contract, on each 20 miles completed; but it is now found that, owing to the character of the work which remains to be done, it would be impossible, with any justice to the Company or to the Government, to carry on that mode of payment. Take the country north of Lake Superior, the whole distance is easy until you come to the 95 miles of enormously heavy work, and, if you paid them *pro rata* according to the contract for the number of miles done, the company would not receive, for the 95 miles a proporate cost of the work. So, in the Rocky Mountains, the 30 miles that is comparatively easy would not bear any proportion to the other work that remained to be done; and it is only proposed to make a change that is based upon the principle upon which payments are made by the Government in relation to almost all the other contracts—I think I may say to all the other contracts, on the canals, on railways, and on everything of the kind—which is to pay for the amount of work done. The whole section from Sudbury Junction, to which the line is now completed, to Nepigon, north of Lake Superior, it is provided shall be covered by a certain sum of money; and, instead of paying for each 20 miles as it proceeds, which, as I say, would leave you without the means of completing the 95 miles of the heaviest portion of the work, it is proposed to adopt the same principle that is adopted in relation to the payments on all similar contracts and almost all the works under the charge of the Government, to pay them *pro rata* as the work proceeds, according to the value of the whole work. In the whole distance there is a certain sum of money to be paid. The Chief Engineer makes his estimate of the cost of the work in order that payment be made for the work done in proportion to its value to the whole; and, having arrived at that conclusion, he gives his certificate that the work done, in regard to that which remains to be done, warrants the payment of a certain sum of money. As 1 have said, it was indispensable, in the interests of the Government as well as in the interests of the Company, that that change should be made, in order to provide *pro rata*, as was the intention, for the work performed by the Company for the Government. Then, Sir, as to the $22,500,000, it is not proposed to pay the company one dollar of it except as the work proceeds, and in instalments proportionate to the value of the work remaining to be done; so that, when the $22,500,000 is exhausted, together with the $12,710,788 of cash subsidy remaining in the hands of the Government, the Government shall have the certainty of the work being completed from end to end. The conditions on which it is proposed to give that advance may be briefly stated in this way. First, there is the charge already described for securing the payment of the guarantee at the end of the five years. Then, there is the forfeiture, upon default of the interest or

principal for twelve months, of the entire property of the
Company. There is the prohibition of any further charge
upon the property, except for the sole purpose of repaying
the advances. It is quite possible—and it may be necessary
more specifically to provide for that, to enable the Company to realize the means of promptly paying the Government, when the opportunity may present itself—it may be
found, in fact, quite desirable to provide that they shall
have authority to establish a charge upon the land
grant, for the purpose of providing the means of wiping out
their indebtedness to the Government, whenever a suitable
opportunity may present itself. Then, there is the removal
from the market of the balance of the $35,000,000 of
stock remaining to be issued. That remains in the hands
of the Government, and, with this entirely under its control,
not a dollar of that stock, even if they provided the amount
as arranged in the first agreement for the guarantee of
3 per cent., can be issued until such time as the Government agree, and then it can only be issued with the
consent of the Government, for the purposes of the road,
or for the purpose of repaying the loan to the Government.
In order to take entire control of that matter, in order to
place the Government in the position that if the value of the
stock rose to a point where we thought it ought to be sold,
and the money returned to the treasury by the Company
that had been advanced, we have power to secure the sale of
that stock and thus recover the amount of indebtedness to
the Government. I need not refer to the proposal to relin-
quish the security of $1,000,000 for construction ; because,
Sir, I need not remind hon. gentlemen opposite that the
object of taking $1,000,000 security for the construction
of $100,000,000 worth of work could only be of one kind,
and that was for the purpose of getting an effective guarantee of the *bond fides* of the Company, and securing ourselves
against the possibility of their failing to go on with the
work. The House knows that in every contract that we
make, as the work advances, it is customary to give up the
security that has been deposited for the construction of the
work—the 5 per cent. security deposited is given up to
the contractors as the progress of the work warrants the
Government in the conviction that the work will be carried to completion. So in this case, seeing that a large
amount of money not received from Government sources
has gone into this work, the Government feel that it would
only be unnecessarily hampering the Company to
lock up, without the slightest cause or necessity, this
$1,000,000 that, to a very large extent, they are
already entitled to receive back according to the

principle we have adopted in contracts of all
kinds with the Government. Now, Sir, I may say
that is the proposal—to postpone with ample security for
its payment already placed in the hands of the Government
by the Company, to postpone the payment of the $7,320,912
for the guarantee, and to advance, as the work proceeds,
$22,500,000. Now, Sir, I will, no doubt, be asked if the
Company have shown the Government that they have a fair
and a legitimate right to ask for that assistance in order to
ensure the completion of this work within two years. And,
Sir, in regard to that matter I will lay before the House a
frank statement of the affairs of the Company, as given by
themselves, which, I think, will remove all doubt as to the
position they have placed themselves in so as to entitle
them to the confidence of the Government in regard to this
application. I propose to give a statement of expenditures
made by the Company, and the sources from which they
have obtained their money and receipts, which, I think, will
satisfy every hon. member in this House how baseless are the
statements that have been made broadcast over this
country, that the moneys received from the Government,
and from Government sources, have been used by the Company outside the contract for the construction of the Canadian Pacific Railway; and that, instead of taking the large,
liberal, and generous subvention that this Government
asked Parliament to provide for the construction of that
road, and putting it into this great work, they have
used those means derived from the Government for the
purpose of engaging in outside enterprises apart from the
Canadian Pacific Railway, and are thus not entitled to come
to the Government and seek for any assistance, even for so
desirable a purpose as that of securing the construction of
this great work five and a half years before the time provided in the contract. The statement placed in my hands
by the Company shows as follows:—

EXPENDITURE.

Works of construction on main line, west of Callander embracing 1,131 miles of completed road		$23,078,929
Works of construction on Branch Lines, west of Callander, embracing 269 miles of completed road—295		3,759,793
Improvements of Government Lines, west of Cross Lake		353,636
Materials, rails and supplies	$4,364,839	
Less advance on rails	339,235	
		4,025,604
Rolling stock	$6,130,792	
Lake steamers	552,251	
Plant tools and outfit for construction	187,002	
		6,870,045
Five per cent. dividend on stock		2,128,000
Interest, &c., on land grant bonds		372,880
Deposit with Government on guarantee		8,710,240

2½

Extension from Callander to Montreal and Brockville......	3,270,351
Rolling stock for above...	900,000
Shops.......	516,032
Tools and machinery..	352,230
Real estate for termiui.. ..	390,790

Total expenditure from Montreal to Kamloops and Brock-
ville............ ....----.. .... **$54,728,500**

*Advances and Accounts Receivable for Extension to the
Seaboard, &c.*

South-Eastern Railway	1,582,327
St. Lawrence and Ottawa Railway.......................................	69,900
Atlantic and North Western do	156,646
Canada North-West Land Company	600,097
Advances to contractors in construction	600,000
Sundry advances and carriers back charges and other	
matters incidental	473,281
Paid in respect of securities deposited with the Government	
in lieu of $1,000,000 cash...........	484,614
	58,695,363

RECEIPTS.

Net receipts from sale of stock	$25,356,828	
Loan on $10,000,000 of stock..........	4,950,000	
Cash subsidy..... ---. ....-.	12,289,212	
Land grant bonds......	9,029,012	
Sale of town sites......-	477,775	
Net revenue $1,115,574 received..................	891,875	
		52,994,702

Excess of expenditure over receipts	$5,700,663
Deduct advances, &c., as above.......	3,966,865
	$1,733,798

Now, Sir, I propose for a moment to review the character of
those expenditures. But before doing so I may be asked;
what evidence I have that this is an accurate statement of
the expenditures and receipts of the Company? And anticipating this question, although of course I was bound to
accept the statement of the Company as a fair and honour-
able exhibit of their actual receipts and expenditure, I felt
it was right, on a matter of so much importance, to be in a
position to give Parliament the most abundant and accurate
information, and to show beyond the possibility of
question that there was no doubt as to the accuracy of the
statements placed in my hands as to the expenditure and
revenue of the Company. And for that purpose the Government nominated Mr. Miall Deputy Minister of Inland
Revenue, one of the ablest accountants in the public service,
and a gentleman who had been employed by the late
Government on financial questions of the gravest importance, as one of the ablest accountants whose services
they could command, to go to Montreal in connection with Mr. Schreiber, the Chief Engineer, whose
familiarity with the whole question would be of

great value in an investigation of that kind, for the
purpose of making such an investigation of the books and
statements of the Company as would assure beyond question the accuracy of the statements they had placed in my
hands. I will read an extract from the report of those
gentlemen, which, I think, will be found to be entirely
satisfactory on that point.

Mr. BLAKE. I suppose the hon. gentleman intends to
lay that report on the Table.

Sir CHARLES TUPPER. I do; I will lay the paper
on the Table. I think, perhaps, Mr. Speaker, as this is an
important paper, I may as well read the correspondence.
The following is the letter addressed by me to those gentlemen :—

"OTTAWA, 28th January, 1884.

"DEAR SIRS,—I have to request that you will, with all convenient speed,
proceed to Montreal, with a view to investigate the books and accounts
of the Canadian Pacific Railway Company so far as such examination
may be necessary to enable you to verify certain statements of revenue
and expenditure which have been laid before my colleagues and myself
by that corporation.

"I am aware that an exhaustive and detailed audit would entail the
labour of weeks, if not months. This is not expected. But you are
required to make such examination as a prudent business man would
desire to make before lending capital to or entering into terms of co-
partnership with a respectable commercial firm. A copy of the Company's statements is transmitted herewith.

"I am, yours faithfully.
(Signed)   "CHARLES TUPPER."

The following is the report made by those gentlemen on
their return :—

"OTTAWA, 2nd February, 1884.

"To the Hon. Sir CHARLES TUPPER, C.B., K.C.M.G.,
"Minister of Railways and Canals.

"SIR,—In obedience to your letter of instruction (bearing date the
28th ult.) we proceeded to Montreal on the morning of the 29th ult.

"On arriving at the offices of the Canadian Pacific Railway Company
we were informed that the President was temporarily absent from the
city; but upon communicating to Mr. Drinkwater the nature of our
errand, he at once placed a room at our disposal, and stated that all
the books, accounts and vouchers would be cheerfully produced for our
inspection.

"He then summoned the Chief Accountant of the Company (Mr.
Ogden) and requested him to hold himself and staff in readiness to furnish any assistance or information required, when we forthwith proceeded
with our investigation. We found the books of the Company under Mr.
Ogden's able supervision, to be faultlessly kept, both as to system and
detail; so that far less difficulty than we anticipated was experienced
in establishing an independent trial balance as the basis of further
operations.

"Working backwards from this point by a process of analysis familiar
to accountants, sufficient detail was obtained not only to check the
figures presented by Mr. Stephen, but also to examine into the details
of each sub-head, where such examination was deemed to be necessary,
and to prove that the general results were arrived at without the aid of

22

any improper manipulation of accounts, directly from the original entries made in proper chronological order from the various subsidiary books.

"We do not wish to convey the impression that the nature of the expenditure under each sub-head has to any considerable extent challenged our attention. Such an examination would, necessarily, occupy a considerable longer time than was at our disposal and would have transcended the limits of our instructions. Neither did we examine into the matter of the distribution of stock.

"As the result of our investigation, however, we have no hesitation whatever in submitting our opinion that the statements furnished by the President and placed in our hands for verification, represent truthfully the actual condition of the Company's affairs as portrayed by the books of the Company.

"It is understood that if any further information is required in respect of specific items, the books are still open to our further scrutiny, whenever you may so determine or require.

"The books of the land grant bond trustees were also placed before us, for investigation, and were found practically to agree with the statement made by the President.

"We have the honour to be, Sir,
"Your obedient servants,
"COLLINGWOOD SCHREIBER,
(Signed) "E. MIALL."

Now, Mr. Speaker, having shown to the House the steps that have been taken to verify the Company's statement, I may ask the indulgence of the House for a few moments while I draw attention to the character of those expenditures. In the first instance, there can be no question as to the expenditure, $23,078,929, on the main line from Callander to the crest of the Rocky Mountains. Then we come to the expenditure of $3,759,793, being for Algoma Branch and Western Division branches, 295 miles being under construction in all. I think, Sir, that there is no hon. member who will not say that in the interests of Canada it would be impossible to find any expenditure to which the Canadian Pacific Railway Company could apply their money more important to the success of the enterprise, more important to the character of the work itself, or of more vital importance to the settlement and development of the great North-West. Every mile of those branches, constructed without any aid whatever from the Government, is calculated, I say, to serve the purpose that the Government had in view in making the contract—the development and advancement of the country, perhaps to a still greater degree in many instances, than a portion of the trunk line itself. I need not detain the House upon this item of $4,025,604 for supplies. These supplies are rails and other materials for the purpose of carrying on the construction of the work. Rolling stock, $5,130,792, is, of course, part of the contract on the main line between Callander and Port Moody, demanded under the contract, and every dollar is expended directly for the purposes for which the contract was made. The expenditure of $552,251 for lake steamers is also an expenditure made for the purpose of facilitating the development of the work of carrying on the traffic and business of the country; and of, at the same time, promoting the construction of the portion which remains to be completed. The plant, tools, and outfit for construction are, of course, incidental to the construction, $187,000, making for that service $6,870,045, upon which, I think, no possible question will arise. Then, we have dividend on stock, $2,128,000, which was, of course, incidental to the sale of the stock, and necessary to enable them to realize the $45,356,828 obtained by the sale of the stock, for the purpose of constructing the road. The interest, &c., paid on land grant bonds, $372,000, was, of course, a necessary expenditure to realize the money they received from the land. The deposit of $8,710,240 with the Government on the guarantee was an expenditure also made directly for the same object as the payment of the dividend on the stock—the object of furnishing money for the completion of the contract. The extension from Callander to Montreal and Brockville, $3,270,351; rolling stock, $900,000; shops, $516,032; tools and machinery, $352,230, and real estate for termini, $390,790, will be admitted, I think, by every person familiar with this question, to be expenditures of the most valuable character to the Canadian Pacific Railway. Every person is aware, Sir, that in the construction of a great trans-continental line, it was of the greatest importance to the character of the undertaking and to its standing, its position, and its success, that instead of commencing at an unknown point, such as Callander—which it would be impossible to make the financial men of the world understand—it was of the most vital consequence to the success of the work, in order to obtain the confidence of the public to carry it on to completion and to make it successful after it was completed—that they should bring that terminus at Callander down to the city of Montreal, where it could be fairly and honestly claimed that there was an inter-oceanic line, extending from the Atlantic communication on the one side to the Pacific on the other. I think, Sir, it will not be necessary for me to say one word to show that, in the interests of Canada and of the Canadian Pacific Railway Company, it was impossible to make an expenditure which was more calculated to benefit the country and benefit the enterprise than the expenditure involved in carrying the terminus from Callander to Montreal. This makes an expenditure upon which, I think, there will be no difference of opinion of $54,728,500. Then, there are further items

24

covering in all the sum of $3,966,865, for advances and accounts receivable; and these stand in a somewhat different position. It is quite true they are embraced, and they may be all held to be fairly embraced, within their charter. It provides for an extension to the seaboard, and the expenditure in connection with the St. Lawrence and Ottawa, and the South-Eastern are for purchases of the bonds of those roads and are, of course, a good asset held by them for the purpose of reaching the Atlantic seaboard. The acquisition of the Atlantic and North-Western charter, and the expenditure under that charter of a considerable sum of money in connecting the Canadian Pacific Railway with the Grand Trunk Railway by a line around the mountain at Montreal, is, of course, embraced within their charter. The expenditure to secure a controlling interest in the South-Eastern Railway was, of course, for the purpose of enabling them to place themselves in a position to draw traffic to the Canadian Pacific Railway, from the Atlantic seaboard, whether at New York, or Boston, or Portland, or St. Andrews, or St. John or Halifax. We, looking at it from the Maritime Provinces, are extremely anxious that they should go to a Canadian port; and I am glad to know that the Canadian Pacific Railway Company attach the greatest possible importance to getting the shortest line to the seaboard that they can, to an open winter port in Canada. The expenditure in connection with that matter—whether by connection with the International Railway, and thus making the shortest line that can be obtained to a Canadian port, open at all seasons of the year—is an expenditure which I believe every person who wishes to see this great trans continental line of railway successful in drawing down traffic and travel from every section of the country, would be only too glad to see them make. It may be said that they aim also at obtaining access to Portland, Boston, and New York. Suppose they do. I say the Canadian Pacific Railway would fail in their duty to the great enterprise in which they are concerned, would fail in their duty to Canada if they did not take every practicable and feasible means of drawing every pound of traffic they can draw from any port in the United States upon a Canadian line to be carried across the continent. Under these circumstances, I say, the expenditure which is made in that regard is one which, I believe, will commend itself to business men—and I am sure it will to railway men—as a sound and prudent consideration. I only regret that they did not when acquiring a railway to the city of Montreal go on to the real ocean port of Canada in summer, the city of Quebec; and I believe that it will be found

necessary by that Company, notwithstanding that
they have reached ocean communication at Montreal
—I believe the interests of the Company will involve
the necessity of their securing direct and complete through communication with the great ocean port of
Canada, for the summer season, at the harbour of Quebec.
I have no doubt that every measure will be taken that can
be taken to attain that important object. I trust that, by
the shortest line to the sea, reaching ports in the Maritime
Provinces by a shorter line than the Intercolonial, and by
connecting the links which have been shadowed forth,
in connection with this matter, they will never rest until they
have come, not only to the harbour of Quebec for summer, but
that, looking to the vital importance of having, as they will
have, a great ocean port there in summer—the great importance of having a Canadian port open throughout the whole
year, winter as well as summer—they will never rest until
they have established a route of communication to St. John,
to Halifax, to St. Andrew's, and ultimately to Louisbourg. I
say, Sir, the fact that when they have reached the harbour of
Louisbourg, the fact that they will make it the interest of
every man who has a letter to send or who wishes himself
to pass in the shortest period of time from London to New
York to go through that harbour, will compel the Company,
in the interest of this great national work, not to rest short
of attaining even that point as the ultimate object. But I
have no hesitation in saying that the distance between
Montreal and Halifax in winter can be so shortened by the
measures that are in contemplation as to give every reason
to believe that the Company will find it their interest, until
Louisbourg is reached, to make Halifax at all times—in
the winter at any rate—the great grain shipping port for the
Canadian Pacific Railway. Now, Sir, with reference to the
$600,000 of stock subscribed by the Canadian Pacific Railway
in the Canadian North-West Land Company, that stands
upon the same footing as many of these other measures. Why
did they subscribe $600,000 of stock in the North-West Land
Company? Every person knows, who has been watching
the proceedings of the Company, that they made a large sale
of land to the Canadian North-West Land Company, and it
was of great moment that the stock of that Company should
be subscribed—should be placed in such a position as
its inherent value deserved, for the purpose of rendering the
Company's land operations successful, and thus giving them
the means for promoting the construction of the Canadian
Pacific Railway. The advance to contractors on construction of $600,000, I understand to stand thus: A con-
struction company was formed, embracing a large number

of the members of the Canadian Pacific Railway Company, if not the Company itself, with a number of outside individuals who were prepared to go into a construction company, and the works were carried on by it. I expect, in response to the application of the hon. leader of the Opposition, to lay on the Table of the House, in the course of to-morrow, the contract with that Company, which will disclose its exact character; but I may say that, so long as the means were found by the construction company and the Canadian Pacific Railway Company combined, to vigorously carry on the work, it was carried on in that way. But, when the time came—when, owing to the stringency of the money market in New York, and the depreciation of the property of the Company, it was impossible to obtain the means to carry on the work—they fell back on the principle of a guarantee in order to obtain funds from another source, and they closed their accounts with the construction company, to whom it appears they had made advances at that time of $600,000. Then there is an item of sundry advances, carriers' back charges, and other matters, amounting to $473,281, which are incidental expenses connected with every great undertaking of this kind. The next amount is the sum of $484,614 paid in respect of securities deposited with the Government, in lieu of the $1,000,000 cash deposit, to secure the completion of the contract. As the House is aware, the Government agreed to release the $1,000,000 in cash, and to accept in its stead, $1,630,000 of Credit Valley Railway bonds. It was found by my predecessor, the late hon. Minister of Public Works and has been found by myself and the hon. Minister of Public Works beside me, necessary—in order to give additional facilities to contractors to complete their work—to exchange the original cash deposit for real estate or a security of some other kind ; and this action of the Government was simply in conformity with the usual plan, adopted by the late Government as well as by this Government, in relation to all other contracts. And I presume—in fact I know—that this payment of $484,614 represented stock belonging to Mr. Stephen in the Credit Valley Railway, and if that deposit is released, this money will go back to the Canadian Pacific Railway Company, to be used in prosecuting the enterprise. Now, Sir, having given as briefly as I could the character of these expenditures, I propose to show a little more in detail how the account will stand. On the main line, between Callander and Port Moody—on the eastern and central sections— with improvements made on the Government line west of Cross Lake, the expenditures have been as follows :—

*Main Line, between Callander and Port Moody, Eastern dnl Central
Sections, with improvements made on the Government Line, west of
Cross Lake.*

EXPENDITURE.

Construction—Nipissing Division			$3,249,971	
do	Lake Superior Division		2,299,783	
do	Western	do	17,529,175	
				$23,078,929
Equipment—rolling stock			$6,130,792	
do	steamers		552,251	
do	tools and plants		187,002	
				6,870,045
Materials on hand—fuel			$459,666	
do	general stores		843,907	
do	rails, ties, &c.		1,539,792	
Supplies for construction			1,521,474	
			$4,364,839	
Less advance on rails			339,235	
				4,025,604
Improvement on Government lines west of Cross Lake				353,606
Five per cent. dividend on stock			$2,128,000	
Interest, &c., on land grant bonds			372,880	
Deposit with Government on guarantee			8,710,240	
				11,211,120
Total expenditure				$45,539,304

CASH RECEIVED.

Cash subsidy paid by Government	$12,289,212	
Proceeds of sales of land grant bonds	9,029,012	
Proceeds of sale of town sites	477,775	
		$21,795,999
Excess of expenditure over receipts		$23,743,305

*Main Line and Branches between Callander and Port Moody, Eastern
and Central Sections, Branches with improvements made on the Government Line, west of Cross Lake.*

EXPENDITURE.

Main line, as before stated		$45,539,304
Branches.		
Algoma Branch	$1,877,324	
Western Division Branch	1,882,469	
		3,759,793
Total expenditure		$49,299,097

CASH RECEIVED.

Main line, as before stated	$21,795,999
Excess of expenditure over receipts	$27,503,098

*Main Line and Branches, between Montreal and Port Moody, Eastern and
Central Sections, acquired Lines, Branches and Improvements, on
Government Line West of Cross Lake.*

EXPENDITURE.

Main line and branches, west of Callander, as before stated	$49,299,097

Acquired lines—

Canada Central Railway	$ 2,251,242	
Q.M.O. & O. Railway	180,853	
Improvements thereon	770,956	
Mile End and Brockville Loop Line Branches	67,300	
		3,270,351
Rolling stock		900,000
Shops—		
Montreal	$362,820	
Perth	115,628	
Carleton Place	37,534	
		516,033
Tools and machinery		352,230
Real estate for termini and shops		390,790
Total expenditure		$54,728,500

CASH RECEIPTS.

Main line and branches west of Callander, as before	$ 21,795,999	
Net revenue—$1,115,574 received	891,875	
		22,687,874
Excess of expenditure over receipts		$32,040,626

Main Line, Branches and Extension, from Seaboard to Seaboard, Eastern and Central Sections, acquired Lines, Branches, Improvement in Government Line, West of Cross Lake, and advances on Lines to the Seaboard, &c.

EXPENDITURE.

Main line and branches between Montreal, Brockville and Kamloops, as before stated		$54,728,500
South Eastern Railway	$ 1,582,327	
St. Lawrence & Ottawa Railway	69,900	
Atlantic & North-Western do	156,646	
Canada North-West Land Co	600,097	
Advance to contractors on construction	600,000	
Sundry advances and carriers for back charges and other matters incidental to traffic, &c...	473,281	
Paid in respect of securities deposited with the Government in lieu of $1,000,000 cash	484,614	
		3,966,865
Total expenditure		$58,695,365

CASH RECEIPTS.

Main line and branches between Montreal and Brockville and Kamloops, as before stated	$22,687,874
Excess of Expenditure over Receipts	$36,007,491
Deduct advances, &c	3,966,865.
	$32,040,626

I trust under these circumstances we have heard the last, either in this House or out of it, of the unfounded statement —as I have proved it to be from the figures that I have submitted to the House—that this Company has taken the money received under this contract from the Government for the purpose of building a line of railway from Callander

to Kamloops and expended it on outside enterprises, apart
from and without any reference to the Canadian Pacific
Railway. If we have not, I think we ought to have reached
that point in the discussion. I may draw the attention of
the House for a moment to the property that is to be covered by the lien. The Canadian Pacific Railway have
property which, if realized at its fair value, is
abundant to complete their contract without any assistance from any source. Having an enterprise on
hand that has established itself beyond controversy
as an enterprise based on a sound commercial foundation,
they are in a position to say that with anything like a fair
realization of the value of the property they possess they do
not require assistance from any person. They are in a
position to say to the Government, we can fall back upon
our contract, we can disband our force of 9,000 men now
operating near Lake Superior, we can draw in our expenditure, and by 1st May, 1891, we shall be enabled to sell land
enough to provide with the net revenue for operating, all that
we require. We shall have the means of completing our contract ; but if you want that great work completed by the
end of 1885, we ask you, not to give us an additional dollar, but to advance to us as the work proceeds the amount
of $22,500,000 for that purpose. I have told the House in
the first place that they do not ask an additional dollar of
subvention for the purpose of completing the contract they
have made w th the Government. I have told the House
that the Company have the strongest confidence in the value of the subvention already given;
that with the amount that can be obtained from the
outside public, and that has been obtained from the outside
public, they have the means of completing their contract.
But while they do not ask the House to give them a single
additional dollar they ask us to use the credit of this
country—which, thanks to the management of my colleague,
the hon. the Minister of Finance, never stood in a
higher position—to obtain the means of accomplishing this
great national work by the end of 1885 ; and that without
imposing the slightest shadow of a shade of additional burthen
upon the Government or upon the country giving security for
the repayment of every dollar by the time the contract was
to be completed, the 1st May, 1891. I say that if this is the
position in which they are—and I think, I may venture to
say, that hon. gentlemen opposite will not controvert
the soundness of that position, will not question the fact
that the security offered to the Government by the Company
for this temporary advance in order to quickly complete this
great national work is abundant—we should not hesitate a

single moment in giving that measure our support.
Let me draw attention briefly to the property that is
covered by this lien by the Canadian Pacific Railway.
I have already said that, if there is either one year's
default in the payment of interest or default in the payment
of the $7,300,000 at the end of five years to cover the
guarantee, or of the amount on the first day of May, 1891,
if, by the first of May, 1892, every dollar of interest and
every dollar of principal is not refunded to the Government
of this advance, they propose that we shall become at once
the possessors of the entire property of the Canadian Pacific
Railway Company. What does that embrace ? That embraces the entire property from the ocean terminus at
Montreal to Port Moody on the Pacific, it embraces the line
on which they have paid over $3,000,000 between Montreal
and Callander, it embraces the line on which they have
expended over $2,000,000 the branch to Algoma
Mills, it covers the 269 miles of branches in the North-West,
it covers the three magnificent steamers that they are
placing upon the route between Algoma Mills and Port
Arthur, and it covers the entire 21,246,000 of acres
of land that remain at the disposal of the Government. I shall not elaborate this question, because I do not
anticipate that any hon. gentleman in this House will say
for a single moment that the security is not so ample, that
the value of the property pledged is not so enormous, as to
place the possibility of failure or the possibility of our not
having every dollar of principal and interest advanced to
this Company refunded, beyond a question of any contingency or of doubt. I may say that this road will embrace,
of the main line from Montreal to Port Moody, 2,886 miles,
it will embrace 112 miles of branches belonging to the lines
between Montreal and Callander, and it will embrace 395
miles of branches in the North-West, making a total of 3,393
miles of road. Let us look for a moment at the character
of that security. The entire charge to which the road
between Montreal and Callander is subject is $5,323,333.
The land grant earned by the Company and unsold
at this moment is 10,002,305 acres, and the land grant un-
earned 11,244,295 acres, or a total land grant to which the
Company is entitled when the road is finished of 21,246,600
acres, over the portion that they have sold. This land is
subject to a lien of $5,000,000, charged as security
for the operation of the road, and, as I have already told
the House, we do not propose in these Resolutions to
release that lien. There is a very great misapprehension, I
find, in some quarters on that point. There is no proposal
in these Resolutions to release that $5,000,000 of land

grant bonds held by the Government as a security for the operation of the line for ten years. I may say that that is rather a matter of sentiment than otherwise, so far as the Government is concerned. We wish the contract to remain intact as we made it, and we, therefore, do not propose to release that lien, although we feel the most confident assurance that it is unnecessary to retain a single dollar of that $5,000,000 of bonds for the security of a road when it is already shown that, with its unconnected portions, labouring under the greatest possible difficulty, its net earnings have been some $978,000 within the last nine months. That the road when constructed will be a valuable property there can be no reason to doubt. That the road this coming year will earn a very large amount of net profit over and above the expenses of its operation there cannot be a question; and, when opened from end to end, it is perfectly obvious that the Canadian Pacific Railway will be placed upon a thoroughly sound and complete commercial foundation, as one of the best lines of railway communication that is to be found in the country. Let us look a little more closely at what this 3,393 miles of road presents. I have already said that the entire land grant of the Company, the 21,246,000 of acres in the hands of the Government, over and above the small portion required to cover the outstanding bonds, will be a security to the Government; and all the money derived from that source will come directly to the Government. The land grant bonds issued are $10,000,000. Of this $6,667,000 have been destroyed or cancelled. There are held by land companies, against instalments of purchase money not yet due, $846,000, making $7,513,000 of bonds that are either cancelled or held by land companies until they make payments on the lands purchased, and they then will come in. That leaves the balance in the hands of the public $2,487,000. The balance of purchase money of land bought by individuals not yet due, applicable to the redemption of this is $1,363,500, leaving a balance of issue not provided for of $1,123,500 in all. So that, when this $1,123,500 of land grant bonds that are outstanding is provided for, the whole 21,246,600 acres of land stand in the position of simply representing securities in the hands of the Government, or money that is to come into their hands as the land is sold. The extent then of the property placed in the hands of the Government is 21,246,600 acres of land and 3,393 miles of road. Suppose an improbable contingency—I will not say improbable—I will say an impossible contingency. There is not an intelligent man in this country who does not know that it is not within the range of possi-

bility, with a lien of such an insignificant character upon a
property of such magnificent proportions as I have shown
this property to be, that any other result can happen than
that every dollar of the principal and every dollar of the
interest will come into the hands of the Government before
a default of twelve months is made. I might dismiss that
subject at once and forever from any consideration,
were it not that it is just as well to look at a phase
of this question that I think has not, perhaps, attracted public attention, and that is, the position the
Government would be in, the position this country
would be in, if this Company made twelve months'
default in the payment of the last dollar of this
money advanced for their assistance, or of the interest
upon it at 5 per cent. Now, Sir, I have spoken of the lands
and the railway. What will that road cost us, assuming
that to-morrow after this arrangement is made, assuming
that to-morrow they make default, assuming that to-morrow
the Company were to abandon the work, what would be
our position? And, Sir, it does not matter whether default
is made now or at the end; the position, so far as these
figures are concerned, will stand the same. I will show you
what this 3,393 miles of road will cost the people of this
country in case of the impossible contingency of default.
I will put the land on both sides of the account, the land
which they have sold, and which netted them $2.36 an acre
on 3,753,400 acres. But, for the purpose of meeting
the views of hon. gentlemen opposite as closely
as I can regarding the value of these lands,
I will call them worth $2 an acre. If we call
the subvention that goes to the Canadian Pacific
Railway Company of 25,000,000 acres of land worth
$2 an acre, it makes, with that which we pay in cash,
and that which we paid in completed road, $103,000,000;
and that, I think, was the favourite calculation of hon.
gentlemen opposite. Now, Sir, I will charge ourselves
with the 3,753,400 acres of land sold at $2 an acre,
making $7,506,800; I charge the advance on rails of
$339,235; I charge the cash subsidy paid, $12,289,212; I
charge the proposed advance of $22,500,000; I charge the
lien on the Canada Central and the Quebec, Montreal, Ottawa
and Occidental Railway, $5,333 333, assuming we will have
to pay it if the road came into our hands; I charge the
guarantee dividend on stock postponed, $7,198,460; I
charge the land grant bonds sold with no sales to redeem
them, $1,123,500; I charge the estimated cost of the work the
Government has to build at $23,000,000; I charge the balance
of cash subsidy, $12,710,788, and what is the total?

I challenge the scrutiny of hon. gentlemen opposite; I will lay this paper on the table, and I invite the closest scrutiny and investigation as to whether this is not a fair statement of the position we would be in if, to-morrow, or at the end of two years, they made default, or if at any period they made default. In regard to this question, I say that is the account; every dollar is charged there that by any possibility the people of this country would have to pay for that 21,246,600 acres of land and 3,393 miles of road, without any charge upon it of any kind from end to end. The whole total is $97,001,328. That is what the road would cost the people of this country. The paper is as follows:—

STATEMENT showing that should the Company fail to fulfil the terms upon which the loan is made, the Goverment will be seized of possession of the following prope·ty for the sums name1 below :—

Extent of Property.

Land ....- · .... 21,246,600 Acres.
Railway and branches .... 3,393 Miles.

Which will Cost.

3,753,400 acres land (sold) say its value at $2 per acre..	$ 7,506,800
Advance on rails	339,235
Cash subsidy paid	12,289,212
Proposed advance of...	22,500,000
Lien on Canada Central and Q.M.O. & O. Ry........ ..	5,333,333
Guarantee dividend on stock postponed	7,198,460
Land grant bonds sold, with no sales of land to redeem them	1,128,500
Estimated cost of Government work .... ,..........................	28,000,000
Balance of cash subsidy	12,710,788
Total	$97,001,328

Assuming the lands to be worth $2 per acre, the following would be the position:—

21,246,600 acres at $2 per acre $42,493,200
3,393 miles of railway at $16,065 54,508,128

Now, Sir, what more? What shall we do with the lands? I have charged the land they have used at $2 per acre, and put it on the other side of the account, and showed equally what the lands have realized, and what our position would be, and what the road would cost us. I credit the road with the 21,246,600 acres of land at $2 per acre, making $42,-493,200 of cash that will come back to us out of the $97,-000,000; and I take the completed road of 3,393 miles without a charge of a dollar upon it, from Montreal to Port Moody, costing the people of this country $54,508,128. That is the total. So, Sir, I say that in that position there is no intelligent man who will say, in the first place, that there is a shadow of ground for supposing that every dollar of this principal, and every dollar of this interest, will not be returned, as provided for in these Resolutions, to the coffers of Canada. And I say, further, that in case of that impossible contingency arising, we would stand in the position after selling the lands-at the value these gentlemen have put upon them, the lands that would come into our hands, we would have the 3,393 miles of main line and branches from Montreal to Port Moody—at a cost to the people of this country of $54,503,128. Well, Sir, what will the Canadian Pacific Railway proper cost us ?—that road, Sir, that hon. gentlemen opposite declared would cost $120,000,000. I need not remind the House that when we were discussing this question before, the hon. leader of the Opposition gave to the House a careful calculation of what it would cost the Government of this country to bui'd a road from Callander to Port Moody, without a mile of branches—the simple line from Callander to Port Moody; and the hon. gentleman stated that he had submitted the careful calculation in regard to this matter to his colleague, the former Minister of Public Works, who had been for years examining this question, and dealing with it as a Minister; and, Sir, these two hon. gentlemen came to the conclusion that the lowest amount for which the Canadian Pacific Railway could be built from Callander to Port Moody was—the hon. leader of the Opposition stated it—$120,000,000. He also submitted the calculation of the hon. member for Lambton (Mr. Mackenzie) my distinguished predecessor, containing the result of that hon. gentleman's most careful and accurate calculation, which put the cost of the road from Callander to Port Moody at, more accurately, $121,700,000, Now, Sir, that is the value of the road, as stated by hon. gentlemen opposite—the lowest cost at which it could be built. It was true, Sir, I had estimated the cost of that line from Callander to Port Moody at $84,000,000, but my hon. friend, the leader of the Opposition, took the opportunity of reminding me that that was not a railway, it was nothing but a tramway. That was after I had stated to the House the character of the road we expected to be able to construct, and I was unable to controvert the statement of the hon. gentleman because it was true. I had stated that, in the position in which we were placed, we had no alternative but to go forward and do the best we could, and I showed that the smallest amount for which we could construct the most inferior line of railway that would give us communication from Callander to Port Moody, would be $84,000,000. I could not controvert the soundness of the hon. gentleman's calculation that the lowest cost for which a railway worth the name — as he called it — could be constructed was $120,000,000, or, to state more accurately the calculation of my distinguished predecessor,$121,700,000.

Now, let us see what that is going to cost the people of this
country under this arrangement :

STATEMENT showing what the main line between Callander and Port
Moody would cost the Government in the event of the Canadian
Pacific Railway failing to repay the loan :

3,393 miles of main line branches and steamers cost...... ...... $54,508,128
The 457 miles of main line and branches between Montreal,
   Brockville add Callander, cost $23,550 per mile,
   amounting to ----- $10,762,736
The 395 miles of branches west of Callander at
   the cost shown by the Company's accounts... 3,759,793
The steamers cost.......... 552,251
                                  $15,074,780

Making a total of $15,074,780, which should be deducted
from the above sum, $54,508,128, to arrive at the cost of
the main line between Callander and Port Moody,
showing the cost to Government of line between
Callander and Port Moody...................... .... $39,433,348

Mr. BLAKE. Hear, hear.

Sir CHARLES TUPPER. The hon. gentleman says
"hear, hear ;" but I will invite him to place his finger upon
the slightest flaw or error in this calculation. I will stake,
Sir, my standing in this House on the accuracy of the
statement I have presented; and if the hon. gentleman can
show that I have not given a fair, frank and unvarnished
statement of the figures and facts as they stand out in the
public records of the country and the documents before the
House, then I will admit that I have no claim to the
confidence of the House in regard to the statement I am
making on this question. I have said there is only one
point which is a question of estimate at all. There are two
points. The one is the estimate that the work with the
supplies on hand can be completed for $27,000,000. Well,
all I can say is that the Chief Engineer of the Department
has gone carefully into that question, and, as the House is
aware, has committed himself to the statement that he
believes the figures of the Company may be accepted as
accurate. With respect to the $28,000,000 of expen-
ditures on works still under construction, I have
given the House the figures down to the present
moment, and I have no reason to believe they
will be, to any considerable extent, increased. But I think
the House will agree with me that there is a great difference between these amounts and $120,000,000, the estimate
of the hon. gentleman opposite (Mr. Blake). And I may
say, in giving the opinions of hon. gentlemen opposite, that
the hon. member for South Huron (Sir Richard Cartwright)
gave, on an important occasion, his estimate, saying there
was no reason to suppose that the construction of the line,

3½

36

oven if due time were given, could be brought within $100,000,000. I think, Sir, I have shown the House that between the estimates of the cost of this work on the part of the hon. leader of the Opposition, the leader of the late Government, and the Finance Minister of the late Government, and this amount of $39,433,348, there is a pretty large margin. Under these circumstances, the line from Callander to Port Moody, 2,511 miles, would cost the people of this country about $15,520 per mile, with ample equipment for service after completion. I need not discuss, I think, at any length, the question of the value of the land. I have placed the value of the lands sold by the Company at $2 per acre against the road, and have credited the Government with the remaining lands at $2 per acre, which hon. gentlemen opposite will not be likely to question. By reference to the speech made by the hon. leader of the Opposition it will be found that he estimated 11,250,000 acres of choice lands— as will be seen by *Hansard*, 1880, page 13—as worth $4.04 per acre, making $45,450,000; at $3.18, $35,775,000 and, addressing your humble servant, he said: " At your miserable $2, $22,500,000." So that the entire amount we are asked to advance to the Company by the proposed Resolutions- -for which there is not other ample security—is covered by the land valued at my miserable $2 per acre, as stated by the hon. leader of the Opposition. So, I think, under those circumstances, the hon. gentleman is not likely to question the accuracy of the calculation which I have submitted to the House in which those lands are placed as worth $2 per acre. On 17th December, 1880, the hon. member for South Huron (Sir Richard Cartwright) gave the House the benefit of his calculation, and (page 16, *Hansard*), he said : " And 18,750,000 acres of selected land worth to-day, as lands are selling in the North-West, at least $37,500,000." And no person knew the value better than the hon. gentleman, because he was giving his attention to that question ; and I am not at all certain, if I had been as free as the hon. gentleman to deal with lands in the North-West, I would not have been alongside him endeavouring to get the benefit of his judgment in making my selections. I am quite certain that from whatever quarter objection may come as to making this advance of $22,500,000 it will not come from that hon. gentleman who has himself declared, so long ago as 1880, before the contract for the rapid construction of the Canadian Pacific Railway was put in operation, when that country was comparatively dormant, when there were 100,000 less people located in the North-West than there are to-day, that

18,750,000 acres of selected lands were worth $37,500,000— that hon. gentleman, I say, will not question the ample character of the security, when instead of 18,750,000 acres we have 21,246,000 acres to cover any advance. There is no doubt that, however valuable the lands were then, they are much more valuable to-day. No person in this country has been more enthusiastic in regard to the value of lands in the North-West than myself. I never was more enthusiastic in regard to their value than I am to day. I say that the value those lands had when the hon. member for South Huron made the speech to which 1 have referred, is much greater to-day, when there are facilities for access, not only by the construction of the trunk line, but by 239 miles of branch lines now in operation in the North-West. Mr. Anglin, your predecessor, said, on the 31st of December, 1880: "If the land is worth anything, if the country is worth settling at all, $2 must be a low average indeed." I may add that, so far as the sales of the Canadian Pacific Railway Company have gone, they fully justify and corroborate the statements made by hon. gentlemen opposite as to the value of the lands, because, on the 3,753,400 of acres already sold, they have received a net price of $2.36 per acre. Now, Sir, I shall not have much more to say in regard to this question, except as to the value of the earnings of the road. I need not say to any person in the least degree acquainted with railway matters that, after all, the vital point, when you come to the question of value, is, what can the road earn? As to the ability of the Canadian Pacific Railway Company to earn money, there was no doubt a large margin for difference of opinion, for speculation, for calculation, as to whether the road would or would not be able to pay its working expenses. I will say nothing of those who were most despondent on that subject, but I will say that those who were most sanguine in this House and out of it, in regard to the character and position of the Canadian Pacific Railway as a commercial enterprise, were not prepared for the evidence which is already furnished, of the fact that all question as to the sound and commercial basis upon which that great national work is placed is completely set at rest. With the evidence already given of the power of the road to earn money, it is settled at once and forever that from this time forward, as the road advances, the receipts will be advanced ; and that when we have this great trans-continental line completed from ocean to ocean we will be in the proud position of finding not only a great volume of traffic and travel drawn over the line, but that the railway will be in a position to make a more satisfactory return than was expected to those who had the enterprise and the courage, when it was a question of doubt, to put their means into this work and grapple with so gigantic an enterprise. I hold in my hand a statement of the gross earnings for 1883; and I find, estimating for the month of December, the amount not to be less than $5,420,931. It is true this includes an amount for the transportation of construction materials and supplies of $1,274,000. But there is no person at all acquainted with the development of the North-West who does not know that the development of that country, which is in its infancy at present, must be in the nature of things very rapid—so rapid that in every ensuing year more will be required in the way of transport to supply the demands of the population by the carriage of freight and passengers than the amount which is charged in this account for the transport of materials. But even deducting that amount and taking the actual traffic revenue, we have a sum of $4,146,913 as against $2,449,824, in 1882, an increase of $1,697,0 9, on the earnings of the road during the past year over the preceding year. Then, as I have already said, the nett earnings of the last nine months, and which I have treated as the receipts of the Company, are no less than $978,660. The announcement of that fact will show the House that the most sanguine expectations of the people who had most confidence in the construction of the Canadian Pacific Railway have been much more than verified by the actual facts as they are now before us. I shall only refer again for a single moment to the enterprise of the promoters. I refer to the gentlemen who originally formed the syndicate of the Canadian Pacific Railway; and I say, Sir, that the very difficulties with which they are now struggling, the very position in which they now find themselves placed, notwithstanding all that energy and enterprise and skill could do, is the best evidence of the courage with which they have grappled with this enterprise. It has been asked what money these gentlemen put into the Canadian Pacific Railway? Well, Sir, I have shown that if you deduct the last dollar received from every source, there is a large balance standing against the Company for money contributed, after all they have received from cash subsidy, from sales of their land and their town sites, from the net profits of operating the line and from all the stock they could sell even at the low price at which it sold—deducting it all, you have a balance still standing against those gentlemen. And what is the fact? Of course there is no syndicate now; the syndicate ceased to exist, when they organized the Canadian Pacific Railway Company and subsequently put the stock of the Company on the open market it then ceased to become their property, and it is now with the shareholders that we have to deal. But I cannot forget that there would have been no Canadian Pacific Railway Company, there would have been no such gigantic progress as there now is if these gentlemen had not had the courage, the energy and the enterprise to risk their own money to the extent of $10,000,000, before asking the people of this country to put a single dollar into the purchase of stock. I say, that they had such confidence in this work that they imperilled their own capital ; and if wo had not had the good fortune to make this contract with men of great wealth, great resources, great energy and enterprise, and great experience, we would have had a most disastrous collapse in connection with this work, and none of the progress and advancement and development which has taken place in connection with the rapid prosecution of this enterprise would not have existed to-day. I do not rest these Resolutions for a single moment on the low ground of any claim that these gentleman have. They have no claim. They made a contract and they received by the terms of that contract a magnificent subvention for the work, great as it was, that they were undertaking to deal with, and they have, no doubt, prospective profits of a large char-acter before them. I do not ask for a moment that these Resolutions shall receive the consideration of the House on any such claim. I say, that if there was no disposition on the part of this House to meet their wishes and their inter-ests in the slightest degree, these Resolutions must stand on the broader foundation of the interests of Canada itself. But, Sir, unless it can be shown, that apart from any claim, those gentlemen have, that, in the interests of Canada, the means should be provided which are required to prosecute this work with the unabated vigour with which it has been prosecuted, then the Resolutions cannot commend them-selves to the House. You will allow me to glance at a few figures—distasteful as they are to myself and to the House —which will show what has been the effect upon Canada of the prosecution of the Canadian Pacific Railway.

It being six o'clock, the Speaker left the Chair.

After Recess.

Sir CHARLES TUPPER. Mr. Speaker, when the House rose at six o'clock, I had drawn attention to the important fact that in case, from any cause, the Company should fail to pay every dollar of the $22,500,000 to be advanced as the work proceeded, and for the purpose of carrying it to com-pletion, or the interest thereon, the people of Canada would obtain the construction of the entire Canadian Pacific Railway—from Callander to Port Moody, for which Parliament provided a subvention (counting the land at $2 an acre) of $103,000,000—for less than $40,000,000 ; and I assumed that that being the case, such a contingency was entirely impossible—that under no circumstances could it be supposed that a Company, possessed of a property which I have shown to be of such immense value, would fail to provide for the payment of a comparatively small sum of money such as' is provided for by these Resolutions : and, assuming that they did pay the money, that Parliament and the country would obtain the construction of the Canadian Pacific Railway on precisely the terms provided in the contract originally made with the Company. I showed further that such was the result of the operation of the line—yielding, as it has, a net profit of $978,660 within the last nine months from the disjointed and disconnected sections of the road, as they now are—that I might assume, as I think I had a right to do, that all question as to the commercial value of the enterprise was entirely set at rest, and that we might fairly come to the conclusion that the Canadian Pacific Railway might be regarded henceforth as placed upon a thoroughly sound commercial basis. I showed on a former occasion that the present Government had adopted the policy of their predecessors in regard to what is called the monopoly in the Province of Manitoba; that when the late Government undertook to carry on the construction of the Canadian Pacific Railway as a Government work, they felt bound to protect the traffic of the road from being drawn off to lines to the south of us in the adjoining Republic, and had consequently refused to issue a proclamation which would charter lines within the Province of Manitoba to connect with American lines to the south. I said that the present Government, when we came into power, adopted that policy; that we felt, as our predecessors did, that, grappling with so gigantic a work as the construction of the Canadian Pacific Railway, we were bound to adopt every possible means of protecting our own line against having its traffic drawn to lines to the south—and, mark you, this was at a time when we did not contemplate at an early day carrying the Canadian Pacific Railway further than Port Arthur. I said further that when we made it obligatory upon the Canadian Pacific Railway Company to extend at once the line north of Lake Superior, giving us an all-rail route from Montreal to the Pacific Ocean, or from Callander to the Pacific Ocean, we felt obliged to give to that Company, upon which we imposed such onerous obligations, all the security that we had considered necessary, and that our predecessors in the Government had considered necessary, for the protection of the Canadian Pacific Railway. But I am glad to be able to state to the House that, although, true to that policy, the Government refused to give assent to the construction of lines within the Province of Manitoba to connect with American railways to the south, such is the evidence presented by the operation of the line so far as it has gone, such is the conclusion arrived at by the Canadian Pacific Railway Company itself in regard to the ability of a through line of the Canadian Pacific Railway to take care of itself, and by the inherent power of its own advantages to maintain its position notwithstanding any competition to which it may be subjected we are now in a position to review and to reconsider the policy of the late Government, and the policy of the present Government, as to the continued necessity for any long period of protecting the Canadian Pacific Railway against competition within the Province of Manitoba, and I am glad to be able to state to the House that such is the confidence of the Canadian Pacific Railway Company in the power of the Canadian Pacific Railway to protect itself, that when the line is constructed north of Lake Superior, the Government feel it will not be incumbent upon them to preserve the position they have hitherto felt bound to preserve, that of refusing to consent to the construction of lines within the Province of Manitoba, connecting it with American railways to the south. I can give no better evidence to the House and the country of the advanced position which we consider this great enterprise of the Canadian Pacific Railway has attained, than when I say that I feel it is consistent with what we owe to the people of this country and to that great national work, that the Government should not deem it incumbent on themselves to pursue the restrictive policy within the Province of Manitoba, which we have hitherto been obliged to maintain. When the House rose, I was about to draw its attention for few moments to the effect the rapid construction of the Canadian Pacific Railway has had upon Canada, and I feel that it will not be wasting your time if, instead of giving you my own opinions in relation to that question or the general public sentiment with regard to it, I should for a few moments call your attention to figures and facts which place, I think, upon a foundation that nothing can shake, the evidence that the progress of Canada, under the rapid construction of this Canadian Pacific Railway, has surpassed anything that the most sanguine promoter of that great enterprise ever could have anticipated. Let me give you a statement of its effects upon the sale of land in the North-

West. Our predecessors were engaged as actively as they felt was in the interests of the public service in the promotion of the construction of the Canadian Pacific Railway. When we succeeded them we felt obliged, in accordance with the opinion we had always professed, to grapple somewhat more vigorously with that work ; but we were not able, down to the time that it was in our power to make this contract with the Canadian Pacific Railway, to take such energetic action as I am glad to know has been taken by that Company since it received the approval of Parliament. I hold in my hands a statement showing the amount received on account of Dominion lands, homesteads, pre-emptions, sales, colonization companies, timber, grazing, minerals and miscellaneous receipts in Manitoba and the North-West Territories, and I asked the hon. Minister of the Interior to divide this so as to show, as far as possible, by contrast, the effect upon this important question of the contract made with the Canadian Pacific Railway. From the 1st July, 1870 to the 30th June, 1880, ten years, we received from all these services the sum of $817,426 ; from the 1st of July, 1880, to the 31st December, 1883, we received $3,572,836, giving the most palpable evidence possible to be given of the effect upon the development of the North-West Territories of the rapid construction of the Canadian Pacific Railway. There is due during the next three years on pre-emptions, since 1880, in addition to the $3,572,836 received since the first of July, 1880, no less than $4,393,070. It would be impossible for me to give to the House more striking, more incontrovertible evidence of the effect upon the development of the North-West Territories caused by the rapid development and construction of the Canadian Pacific Railway, than that furnished by the statement I have just submitted. Then, if you turn to the Department of Customs, what is the effect shown there upon the trade of that country by the rapid construction of the Canadian Pacific Railway? In 1880, the Customs receipts in Manitoba were $279,766, and in the North-West Territories, outside of Manitoba, $21,856; or a total receipt of Customs revenue in the North West, including Manitoba, of $319,622. In 1882, the Customs receipts in Manitoba were $1,054,601, and in the North-West Territories, $51,755, or a total of $1,106,356. In 1883, they had risen from $297,000, in 1880, to $1,764,805 in Manitoba, and $68,137 in the North-West Territories; or a total of $1,832,942, in 1883, as compared with $319,622, in 1880. It would be impossible for any evidence to establish more conclusively the enormous and rapid development of any country, consequent upon any action taken by a Government, than these figures

establish. The total amount of duty collected in Manitoba and
the North-West Territories from January 1st, 1881, to December 1st, 1883, was $1,831,167 more than the total sum col-
lected from June 30th, 1870, to December 31st, 1880. So
that you have the striking evidence of a single year covering a larger amount of duties than the ten years previous.
Now, Sir, I will draw your attention for a moment to the
evidence given by another Department of the public service
—that of Inland Revenue. It will hardly be necessary for me
to allude to the fact that, under an Act which I had the
honour of submitting to Parliament when Minister of Customs, in 1873, the Inland Revenue Department has not much
to do, I am happy to say, in the North-West Territories,
because, under that Act, we established what is called a
Maine Liquor Law throughout the North-West Territories,
which prevents the manufacture or sale of intoxicating
liquors in any part of those Territories. The result of that
enactment has abundantly justified it. It was with no small
degree of satisfaction that I found, when it was proposed to
take a section of the North-West Territory within the bounds
of old Manitoba, that the people arose *en masse* against it,
and protested against being carried into the Province of
Manitoba on any other terms than that they could maintain
the exclusion of intoxicating liquors which they then
enjoyed in the North-West, and retain that provision when
they became part of the Province of Manitoba. But in that
Province, as you are aware, the Excise Department has had
something to do, and the Excise revenue of 1879-80, was
$65,841, with $1,567 for stamps in addition to Excise. The
Excise revenue rose from $65,000, in 1879-80, and $96,000, in
1880-81, to $184,750, in 1882-83, and to $84,257 in the first
six months of the fiscal year from July 1st to December 31st
1883. From 1873-74 to 1879-80, six years, the Excise collected was $215,000, whereas, from 1880-81, to December
31st, 1883, two years and a half, it was $530,328. Then, if
we come to another indication of the condition of the people,
and a very striking indication of the condition of the masses
of the people, the balances at the credit of depositors in the
Government Savings Bank at Winnipeg, we find additional
evidence of prosperity. On December 31st, 1880, there
were balances of $153,589. On December 31st, 1883,
the balance had risen to $615,351, an increase since the
contract was ratified with the Canadian Pacific Railway
Company of over $400,000 of balances due to depositors in
the Savings Bank. Then, if you take the evidence which
the Post Office Department affords, you find the like
gratifying indication of the remarkable progress of the
country. I hold in my hand a statement showing the

amount of mail matter posted at offices in Manitoba and the North-West during the period of one week in 1881, 1882 and 1883, and I am obliged to confine it to one week because I could not obtain the same general statistics in that Department as I was able to obtain in the others. In a single week in 1881, the letters and post cards mailed were 42,394, and the newspapers, books and samples, 6,552. For a week in March, 1882, there were 62,892 letters and post cards mailed, and 12,053 newspapers, books and samples. For the corresponding week in March, 1883, it had risen in a single year from 62,000 to 89,847, with 18,193 newpapers, books and samples. The money order business in Manitoba also exhibits a very striking illustration in the same way. The issues of money orders in 1875 were $26,452.85; in 1876, $29,139.73; in 1877, still less, $28,350.25. In 1878, when of course the change of Administration gave new life and impetus to the people, they rose to $46,751, in 1879 to $69,986, in 1880 to $172,396, and in six months to the 31st December, 1880, to $107,101, making a total from the 30th June, 1875, to the 31st December, 1880, of $480,000 issues of money orders in Manitoba. The amount of money order business done in Manitoba and the North-West Territories from the 1st of January, 1881, to the 31st December, 1883, was as follows: For the six months ended June 30th, 1881, $114,270; for the year ended June 30th, 1882,$398,241; for the year ended June 30th, 1883,$677,722; and for the six months ended December 31st, 1883, $347,854. From the 30th June, 1875, to the 31st December, 1880, the total issues were $480,000, while in the six months ended the 31st December, 1883, they amounted to $347,000, or nearly as much as in the whole of those previous years, and the total from the 1st January, 1881, to the 31st December, 1883, was $1,538,088. Now the most striking illustration perhaps of all, the most striking evidence of all of the rapid development of the North-West, that in which we are all the most interested, is the number of immigrants that we are enabled to attract into the country. We all know that we have in Manitoba and the great North-West Territories an unbounded field for development. We all know that in that country we have the great remaining wheat region not only of British North America but of the continent itself. We all know that Mr. Consul Taylor, the American Consul for the last twenty years at Winnipeg, and a high authority, has publicly declared that three-fourths of the wheat area of North America lies to the north of the boundary line. We all know, in the first place, that the soil of that country exceeds in fertility the soil of any part,

I may say, of the known world—certainly there is in the
wheat bearing States to the south of us no parallel to be
found to the fertility of the soil in the Canadian North-
West. We know now, Sir, that we have 250,000,000 acres
of magnificent farming lands that for fertility cannot be
surpassed on any portion of the civilized globe. But, Sir,
notwithstanding that we have that unbounded field for
development, we were able to accomplish but little, and we
never would have accomplished much, towards its development, but for the construction of the Canadian Pacific
Railway. Now, Sir, the best evidence we have that
at this moment the eyes of the world, the eyes of
those who, in the older and more thickly populated
countries of Europe, are looking for a newer and better
field for their labour and their exertions, is what is taking
place now across the water. We know that their
eyes are concentrated upon the North-West of Canada as
they never would have been, and never could have been
concentrated, but for the construction of a Canadian Pacific
Railway. And, Sir, we know, not only that we have a field of
boundless extent for development, but that in addition to
the fertility of the soil, the character of the wheat that is
grown in that northern clime surpasses in excellence the
character of the wheat that can be grown in any southern
or more genial clime. So, Sir, from every point of view
from which we may be pleased to look, we see boundless
possibilities in that country. We all regard every means
for the development of that country as the means, and the
only means, by which Canada can rapidly become a great and
prosperous country, and attain such a position as every true
Canadian must desire to see her attain, and that at a very
early date. It would be impossible to over-estimate the
effects that this rapid construction of the Canadian
Pacific Railway and the measures taken by that Company to diffuse throughout the world information in regard
to that country, have had in drawing immigration into it.
Now, Sir, let me give you the figures touching immigration, and what do they show? Why, Sir, they show
that the total number of persons who entered the North-
West during the ten years previous to letting the contract
to the Canadian Pacific Railway Company, that is, from
1871 to 1880 inclusive, was 64,755. The total number who
entered the North-West since the contract with the Canadian
Pacific Railway Company was signed, that is, during 1881,
1882 and 1883, is no less than 149,560 immigrants. The total
value of the money and effects brought to the Dominion—
and that is an entirely secondary consideration to that
which is more valuable than money—that industry and

labour which is necessary to create great national wealth—I
say, even in that regard there is great progress, for the total
amount brought in by settlers in 1875 to 1880 inclusive, as
nearly as it can be ascertained in six years, was some
$6,000,000; while during the past three years the sum taken
into the North-West, at the lowest ra'e, can be placed at
over $15,000,000. I leave these figures to the House as
evidence of the effect produced in the development of the
North-West Territories by the rapid construction of the
Canadian Pacific Railway. Now, Sir, a very important
point in connection with immigration is the cost of carrying immigrants into the North-West. The first question
asked by an immigrant in any part of the Continent of
Europe or in Great Britain, when he proposes to come to
this country is, what is the cost of being able to get
there? And the question of a few dollars in the difference of
cost very frequently, as any gentleman who has any know-
ledge of the subject knows, diverts the immigrant from one
line to another. Now, Sir, the published charge on the all-
rail route from Quebec to Winnipeg, at the present moment
is $31.50; the charge *via* the lakes and Duluth on the
route from Quebec to Winnipeg is $25.50. The figures
I have given are those that prevailed for some years,
but an arrangement that has been in operation for
the last two years, has reduced the charge from Quebec
to Winnipeg to $21.64, and *via* the lakes and Duluth
to $16.64. I believe, Sir, these rates have never been pub-
lished. But, in consequence of the rapid progress made by
the Canadian Pacific Railway Company, it is now in our
power to say to the immigrants on the Continent of
Europe, and in the British Isles, that the rate from Quebec to Winnipeg, *via* Port Arthur, will be reduced this
spring from $31.50 to $12, and from Montreal to Winnipeg,
via Port Arthur, to $10. I need not say to the House what
an enormous impetus this change in the cost of carrying
immigrants into that country will naturally produce upon
the volume of immigration that will be thrown into it.
I desire, Sir, to say a single word here in regard
to a point that has attracted some attention in a portion of
the press of this country, and that is: that an arrangement has been made at a comparatively low rate for immigrants coming *via* New York, over the Erie Railway, and
making connection at Brockville, thus reaching Winnipeg
via the port of New York, at an unprecedentedly low rate.
I may say, Sir, that the Canadian Pacific Railway Company had nothing whatever to do with that arrangement.
My hon. friend, the Minister of Agriculture, is responsible
for that arrangement; and I will make a statement to the

House that will satisfy every man in Canada that he would
altogether have failed in his duty to the country if he had
not adopted that course. Every person will acknowledge
the immense importance of reducing the rate for immigrants
from Quebec to Winnipeg from $31.50, the published rate,
down to $12. Every person will see at a glance the enormous
tide of immigration that will be brought into that country
by that change. But, Sir, there was this difficulty, that if
you made that low rate by the steamers to the port of
Quebec, and did not provide for a correspondingly low rate
to the port of New York, the effect would have been this:
At this moment, as you are aware, on the Continent of
Europe, all the emigration service is performed by agents
of steamships lines, and the moment that the rate was
cutd own to that low figure by the lines of steamers to
Quebec, and there was not a corresponding reduction by
New York, you would enlist the services of every emigration agent on the Continent of Europe and throughout
Great Britain also, who was in the interest of the lines
of steamers running to New York—not against the Canadian lines of steamers—for they dare not do that, but to
denounce and decry Canada, as the only means by which they
could serve the interest of the steamers sailing to New
York. It thus became absolutely essential in the interests of
Canada that we should have not only this low rate of
passage and this communication from Quebec, but that in
order to retain our hold, and to strengthen our hold, which
we are most anxious to do, upon the immigration from the
Continent of Europe, we should prevent that which was
otherwise inevitable, and that was that every agent for
every line of steamships sailing to New York from Great
Britain or the Continent, would from Monday morning
to Saturday night, year in and year out have been de-
nouncing Canada for the purpose of holding immigration to
the port of New York. Under these circumstances, I am sure,
Sir, there are no men in this country who would not feel that
our policy was in the interests of Canada and in the
interests of Quebec, for the moment you set every immigrant
agent on the Continent of Europe against this country
and thus prevent people coming by the Canadian lines
of steamships, you take most effective means to prevent the
great tide and volume of immigration which, under
existing circumstances, will naturally flow to Canada
through the port of Quebec. Of course, we all know the
importance of saving the distance as well as lowering the
rate. Men who were obliged to go by Chicago to Winnipeg
had not only to pay $31.50 instead of going through Can-
ada for $12, but they were obliged to run the gauntlet of a

long journey through the United States, during which every possible inducement would be used by agents of land and railway companies to prevent them ever reaching the Canadian North-West. That is one of the great objects attained by the rapid construction of the Canadian Pacific Railway. That is one of the great objects attained by the Canadian Pacific Railway Company in obtaining a line from Montreal through to Winnipeg, and in that way we have not only avoided exposing immigrants, who would otherwise be liable to be taken off our lines to other sections, by carrying them by a route entirely through Canadian territory, as they will be carried next spring; but they will avoid a circuitous journey of 500 miles longer and be taken by a direct line from Quebec to Winnipeg, through our own territory instead of round by Chicago. I want to place a very condensed calculation before the House in respect of the capabilities of the North-West. I am not going to deal with the question of a little difficulty that has occurred in consequence of the frost during the past season. It has been greatly magnified, greatly to the disparagement of the North-West and Canada. But they had frost in Ontario, Dakota and Minnesota, and even in New York State, and those who were not fortunate enough to get their crops in early have suffered to a greater or less extent. It only requires a little more prompt and energetic action on the part of the farming population in getting their crops in early in spring to avoid any contingency of that kind in the future, and of course it was an entirely exceptional year. But I may say that I believe there are few members of this House, much as our attention has been turned to the development of the North-West, who have begun to contemplate in all its fulness what the capabilities of that great country are. I have spoken of its enormous extent, of the unexampled fertility of the soil, of the splendid description of wheat that can only be produced in these more northern and colder climes. But let me just ask the attention of the House for a single moment to a few figures which will indicate what the capabilities of that country are in regard to the production of wheat. One hundred thousand farmers, each farmer cultivating 320 acres of wheat land—has any hon. member made the calculation of what they would produce?

Sir RICHARD CARTWRIGHT. Yes.

Sir CHARLES TUPPER. I am glad the hon. gentleman has done so. I am glad his attention has been drawn to the fact that 100,000 farmers cultivating 320 acres each, or

200,000 farmers cultivating half that quantity each, and taking the product at only 20 bushels to the acre, instead of 27 or 30, which is the average in the North-West in favourable years, would give 640,000,000 bushels of wheat, or 50 per cent. more wheat than the whole United States produces to-day. You have only to look at those figures for a single moment to see what the future of Canada may be to see what a magnificent granary for the world is placed in our Canadian North-West; and when you remember we have six belts running through that fertile country that would each give 320 acres each to 100,000 farmers, you can understand to some little degree what a magnificent future awaits us in the development of that great country. And, Sir, I say that I believe Canada has just reason to be proud of the fact, and all history will give credit to the people of this Dominion, because they had the courage, the daring I may say, to grapple with the construction of a Canadian Pacific Railway. Sir, when the United States had a population of over 38,000,000, the world was astounded at the fact that they undertook to secure the construction of a trans-continental railway. It attracted the attention of the civilized world, and day by day it was heralded in the press as an astounding fact, that the United States had undertaken to construct the Union and Central Pacific Railway. Why, the Union and Central Pacific all told were nothing like as long as the Canadian Pacific Railway. The Union and Central Pacific only covered some 1,900 miles of road, while the Canadian Pacific Railway proper covers 2,541 miles; and yet four and a half millions of Canadians, which we were then, had the courage to undertake a greater work than that which was undertaken by 38,000,000 of people in the United States, and which attracted the admiration of the world. I say, and I say it fearlessly, that history does not furnish to-day an example of a more courageous, a more daring and more remarkable enterprise than that which was undertaken by the Government of Canada, when they said: We have a magnificent North-West to develop. We have a great country, half of the continent of North America, placed under our control and management, and for which we are responsible; and with these responsibilities we will do and dare what only men who feel that they can rely confidently upon the resources of a great country, half a continent, ought to dare and undertake; and if the present generation do not give us credit for it, in all time to come it will be regarded as one of the greatest accomplishments of the century in which we live, that we had the vigour and daring to grapple with that great enterprise. Providence has favoured us. God and nature have marked out on the face of the Can-

4

adian Dominion the shortest and best route for a trans-continental line of railway. Providence has marked out and placed within our borders and within our reach a line of communication from ocean to ocean, the shortest that can be found, a shorter connection between the east and the old world than any other. Providence has placed within our borders a line of railway, a larger portion of which runs through a more fertile country than is to be found on the continent of America. Providence has placed in our hands and under our management a line of railway in which the pass through the Rocky Mountains is lower, the Rocky Mountain section is shorter, and the snow-fall is lighter than on either the Northern or Union and Central Pacific. This road, when completed, makes it shorter for a man living in Chicago—to say nothing of our own people—who wishes to reach the Pacific Ocean, to take the Canadian Pacific Railway by the nearest approach he can obtain and pass to Port Moody, thereby obtaining a shorter line of travel than he could take to San Francisco within his own country. Under these circumstances the Government of Canada have discharged what they believed to be their duty to their country in grappling as they have grappled with this great question. I say, Sir, with the evidence that we have before us of the unexampled and unprecedented development which has followed our efforts in this regard, we would be faithless to our obligations and to our country if we neglected to adopt the means which are now propounded for the consideration of Parliament, of accomplishing the rapid and early completion of that great national enterprise. I know too well how thoroughly this question of the Canadian Pacific Railway has sunk into the hearts and minds of the people of Canada, to have the slightest doubt or hesitation in assuming that this Parliament will, on the present occasion, as it has on previous occasions, give a hearty and generous response to the proposal of the Government. We would be unworthy the position we occupy—the advanced position we occupy on this Continent in regard to this great national measure—if having put our hands to the plough we were to turn back, or for a single moment shrink from the plain and obvious duty which devolves upon us of carrying this great national work to completion at the earliest possible moment in our power. We have obtained a position in the estimation of the mother country and of the world, we have obtained a status by the rapid construction of this gigantic enterprise that Canada could not have obtained in twenty years by any other means. With that fact, patent and lying on the surface, in regard to this great question, the people of Canada will demand at our hands that when the opportunity presents itself of obtaining without the cost to the country of a single dollar of additional subvention, the completion in two years of a work which otherwise would take until 1891—they will demand that without hesitation we should, in the interests of Canada adopt the course which is indicated in these Resolutions. As I said before, I ask this not in the interests of any body of gentlemen—not in the interests of the Canadian Pacific Railway Company—I ask it, Sir, from this House, as the people of this country will demand it from us in the interest of the country to which we belong, in the interest of Canada of which we are so justly proud.

www.ingramcontent.com/pod-product-compliance
Lightning Source LLC
Chambersburg PA
CBHW031813090426
42739CB00008B/1252